# Want for Nothing

Published by Slope Editions, Greenfield, MA

Distributed by Itasca Books

Publisher's Cataloging-in-Publication Data

Names: Woodward, Jon, 1978-, author.
Title: Want for nothing / Jon Woodward.
Description: Greenfield, MA: Slope Editions, 2026.
Identifiers: ISBN: 9781733569736
Subjects: LCSH Poetry. | American poetry. | BISAC POETRY / General
Classification: LCC PS3623.O685 W36 2026 | DDC 811.6--dc23

First Edition
Printed in the USA
Cover art: *A Thousand Plateaus, Chapter 1: Paragraph 6* by Marc Ngui
Design by Ben Pease

slopeeditions.org

# Want for Nothing

Jon Woodward

SLOPE EDITIONS

# Table of Contents

# Introduction

Jon Woodward's *Want for Nothing* is an inventive and compulsively readable book about what is happening to language right now.

Structured in three five-line stanzas with lines of six words each, each line hinged on a caesura at the center, and unfolding in 8 parts, *Want for Nothing* achieves an effect almost like pixelation, such that images and phrases pour forth seemingly "naturally" all the while pulsing their sensation and music through a meshwork, a grid that reflects the fiber optics, tracked metadata, and quasi-carceral irrigations of social connection and human mind through which we lately do all – or almost all – of our imagining.

The speaker is a climber – a rock-climber, I think – conjuring movement out of the reified, computery stasis we all know – because it is socially inculcated. *Want for Nothing* unspools against not only the old interdictions about the barbarity of poetry "after Auschwitz," but the crushing sense of language's futility *in the midst* of genocide.

All this is fine – but what makes Woodward's book special, innovative, unique, and even astonishing – is the fact that he has found a way to *move* relentlessly forward while meditating in an – in our – Emergency.

*Want for Nothing* feels rooted in the New York School – it does this and it does that – "skipping the informal / lunchtime seminar on      bryophytes to write / imperceptible formalist poetry      inspiring if true" bearing witness to stasis and liberty of mind simultaneously.

"I get the    glimmers," he writes, "a speaking / feeling English just diurnal English comes / decoupled I'm speaking." These glimmers, I think, are the same frolicsome and magic *something* Wyatt and Surrey found out about when *they* played around with ordinary English, such as it was in their day, till it decoupled from mere utility, and turned instead toward the expansion of consciousness – the sonnet – even, dare I say, toward bliss.

Poetry must give pleasure. I forget who said this. Was it Pound? Wait a second, I'll look it up – it wasn't Pound (thank God). It was Wallace Stevens who said that poetry must give pleasure, and he was right – and this is something I think it gets easy to forget. Partly, I suppose, because it can feel "barbaric" (alright, that's Adorno) to give pleasure while the culture wallows in a moral abyss.

I don't have a moral answer to this conundrum, but what I do know is that *Want for Nothing* seems to move into and against the notion that a speaker (a poet) could possibly exist who lacked nothing, who needed nothing, whose verse stayed latent in their mouth (or hand), whose egg or seed led to no child, some kind of self-contained and risk-free violence-free lifeform with nothing to bear witness to and no one to bear witness *for*.

Here is Woodward translating Adorno, or should I say Celan: "speech is impossible    I'm a boxcar / was buried alive    as a neonate / your constant demand    your market pressure / to speak sincerely    with plausible affect...."

Yeah. Speech really does feel impossible right now. Authentic speech, poetic speech. And the gambit that Poetry itself presents to us, the *dare*, is to find a way to live, to move nevertheless.

So. This is a poetics of flow. Woodward's caesurae form and forge synaptic leaps: its neopastoral is neurological – less leaping stags than sparks of mind whose apparent levity feels like the only route to – forgive the socially-exhausted word – authenticity.

Woodward's lines do something new – very difficult to do – with their own music: his poems make poetry feel new. (OK, that *is* Pound.)

Reading his compulsively readable and actually *fun* book, I found myself reflecting on what American poetry was when the Modernists invented it.

To refresh: Pound said translations must make their source material *new*, but the very idea of making old things new was modern – which is to say, antique.

Williams was the mystic who went beyond the merely new into a shocking and less commodifiable realm: the *present*. His poetics, especially as elaborated in *Spring And All*, had to do with catching the sense of immanence and excitement that flickers somehow behind and beyond language, but that we most readily access *through* language. Williams dislodged the word from the bilious humors and melancholy that had previously yoked it; kept it in service. He made *the present moment* matter more than empires, traditions, collectively-consented-upon-realities, or anything. He re-gave birth to *Spring*.

*Want for Nothing* is a refreshment of the art form. Its silly, oneiric, relaxed good nature, sweet as Marvell, witty as Smart, "femur humerus years / spilling into aeons   of fresh flowers" achieves a kind of greening – Viriditas – and now I'm quoting Hildegard von Bingen – in the mind of any data-addled reader. "one reads what / data doesn't say   does data nest / inside data deeper   than one museum...."

After all, poetry is *not* a museum – a curation of dead, if gorgeous, artifacts. Poetry, like water – like money, I'm told – must flow. *Want for Nothing* brims with generosity so casual one can almost miss its seriousness. "I thought maybe    I'd rewrite the / constellations for you.../ when you / look up at    night you could / see the changes    waiting to be / written for you    or by you"

– for nothing need be as it was, or is. Please enjoy this.

-Ariana Reines

# MOUTH SPEAKING

the two watches     were in sync
to the second     now they're not
they're exactly off     the seconds' thresholds
pass as meaning     passes as confetti
rain of confetti     love of confetti

maybe he's asleep     and writing again
the mockingbirds gave     him 12¢ change
and a naked     lady baseball card
how am I     supposed to have
written this he     asks in mockingbirdese

tears flow downhill     from the sky
crossing occurrence's kingdom's     threshold ticking ticking
bereftness into sequence     "a new heaven"
"a new earth"     you think that
you can front     when revelation comes

everything's fine just      doing some e-commerce
with half a      frosted blueberry Pop-Tart
hanging out of      my mouth like
a Hunter S.      Thompson cigarette I'm
just back from      Gainesville where sweet

moron after sweet      moron convinced me
in ways no      craft ever could
how completely fucked      a 2024 is
so I'm just      skipping the informal
lunchtime seminar on      bryophytes to write

imperceptible formalist poetry      inspiring if true
I'm just elbowing      a stack of
folders off my      desk earlier during
a careless chair      swivel after simultaneously
answering twelve of      tomorrow's sentient emails

a small child     wrapped in a
green fleece blanket     with cartoon monsters
on it being     loaded into the
back seat of     one of those
shapeless cars and     a procession of

people mostly wearing     dark clothing with
mostly dark hair     or hats one
block over one     block ago now
this block they've     turned into redbuds
and trash cans     actors are students

of human behavior     but you never
see one staring     awkwardly at nothing
while thinking of     something else like
our neighbor's surveillance     cat just caught
me doing by     the bike shed

me not wanting    to "devastate" people
with the speaking    mouth trick that
polished syntax that    speechy luster that
characteristic charismatic poignant    self-involved springtime loveydovey
geargrinding flowercore that    puckish coquettish sincerity

then life took    a couple shits
in my mouth    and looking around
I feel lucky    it wasn't worse
I thought why    not manipulate these
people it seems    to bring them

comfort why not    just stand on
the "devastate" button    feeding them wormwood
chiffon pie painting    their little serotonin
receptors by number    and hole-punching the
silence they crave    through their forehead

I'm one of      those flight attendants
who's always pacing      up and down
the aisle mouthing      big exaggerated shapes
of phonemes at      people in the
coasting silence so      I don't wake

anybody up yelling      this about the
plane or that      about the plane
I'm realizing maybe      it's something like
instructions I'm mouthing      I know you
know about that      thing I have

for being obeyed      in a consenting
and mutually affirming      context of course
and plane crashes      notwithstanding or it's
some gray gremlin      mouthing through me
and there's nothing      to be done

speech is impossible      I'm a boxcar
was buried alive      as a neonate
your constant demand      your market pressure
to speak sincerely      with plausible affect
a talkbox made      of a voicebox

you don't exist      your concerns are
scale models demonstrating      only as much
but you're welcome      to come inside
the camera lucida      its own framed
frame photograph a      simple blank box

speech bubbles bespeak      speech's dead zones
outside the walls      it's dead dirt
or alive again      saying to you
such untrue things      you want truth
to claim life      which speaks true

sitting out front      on the stairs
I was looking      through a droplet
of saltwater at      magnified pixels sharpened
somehow even as      they were bent
a little the      blue black was

split from the      red black on
either side of      the curve of
a silent e      more droplets landed
on the screen      half of me
went back inside      half stayed put

wondering what it      would say if
suddenly you sat      on the stairs
beside it it      couldn't decide if
an apparition could      be told the
truth or even      shown the phone

your arms are     arms like mine
you say to     me "bubble me
up" and I     laugh like no
future ever was     why's it funny
toys figures phrases     injection molded seam

along either side     when I wake
up the words     come instantly apart
I get the     glimmers a speaking
feeling English just     diurnal English comes
decoupled I'm speaking     from inside a

tree made of     wasps I dreamed
I'd wake up     where are you
are you there     nothing answers I'm
awake already sobbing     this was 2015
I wish I'd     kept better notes

in this one   I'm some sort
of slime monster   in this one
I'm standing on   top of Independence
Monument in this   one I'm abandoning
myself someone I   loved just slapped

me across the   face as punctuation
and I'm withdrawing   to a secret
spectator's area which   works as evidence
almost when it   happens again that
I deserved it   in this one

I'm piling my   bike drunk up
onto a parked   car in this
one I'm opening   a shoebox time
capsule I made   in 1991 in
this one I'm   trying on eyeglasses

# HEAR ANYTHING

without hearing anything     of myself without
the backhoe silently     ripping up asphalt
without my Botticelli     Birth of Venus
socks that Anne     gave me hiked
up past midcalf     to bottle my

gnarlying veins without     my comfortable black
canvas shoes without     my butterscotch aviator
sunglasses without my     Portland Sea Dogs
T-shirt without the     scent of apple
blossoms up my     nose so unlike

apples as Sam     pointed out without
even the oxygen     in the air
in every corner     of my lungs
without a cloud     in the sky
without a care     in the world

this time last    year I was
obsessed with "Infest    the Rats' Nest"
the fully depleted    Metallica schtick the
squalid cutpaste guitar    solos reifying the
dead end snarled    in the amber

on Venus I    don't have an
album of spring    2024 yet I'm
on a bench    by the Mystic
behind the Schrafft's    building listening to
the constant effort    of not hearing

my very vanilla    tinnitus turns 28
this year my    own cosmic stylophone
with its stylus    welded across its
entire upper end    somewhere among the
blunt brown smokestacks    across the river

it can't be that hard to
make those cringey feedback sounds with
your guitar it sounds the same
every time and performs moreover the
same expando-foam function in the composition

this is my challenge one year
no feedback I call it the
one year no feedback challenge hey
rock stars what do you think
are you with me rock stars

things you could do instead include
seeing to the generous general provision
mitigating losses of biodiversity and habitat
edifying the interior cosmos reckoning and
recapitulating the balance of the void

my social self    I'm a delight
go ask anyone    I'm friends with
the extinction event    of the summer
makes people glad    that Jon's here
ask that rabbit    kitten budding from

my chest screaming    discovering itself alive
woke me up    a sound it
turned out was    the window fan
mixing with my    own ears ringing
a blister liquid    awake afraid of

anything that symbolic    I didn't cum
since yesterday so    I'm carrying that
around too a    teaspoon of nobody
waiting for its    glimmer of daylight
its moment to    be a delight

# WANT FOR NOTHING

I decided I      would wear nothing
but butterscotch sunglasses      and a suit
of octopus leather      the grottoes blossomed
handwritten sexual overtures      in lunar gravity
which is all      well and good

but you know      me I'm trying
to plumb into      cognition's mysteries and
such and half      of me's like
but peacock IS      mystery while the
other half's already      cocking back the

backswing of a      big (even for
me) braided self      lacerational bullwhip so
fine I eat      the sunglasses I
turn the dial      on the suit's
brain to "unexceptional      guy" problem solved

I'm like one      of those flight
attendants who sits      quietly in the
corner of Gorilla      Adventure at the
zoo holding on      to a secret
nothing special a      hand of cards

a D20 roll      a hide or
a seek I      won't share it
because you wouldn't      share it and
the gorillas don't      care and the
zoo doesn't know      I'm here and

the airline's not      trying to get
me out because      they don't want
a bunch of      copycat flight attendants
slipping away to      the zoo unnoticed
to play some      endless pointless game

his nuts never really worked right
sometimes they made confetti sometimes they
made peppermint silly string sometimes fun
party favor noises the doctor sighed
and said just keep doing what

you're doing and he was like
so just keep jerking off 1.5
or like 1.8 times a day
on average and the doctor said
that can't be the entirety of

what you're doing it was true
normal thoughts formed normal thoughts formed
within normal thoughts a little decorator
crab or what's that clam called
that does that same decorator behavior

you never will    but you could
pick me like    a dandelion your
summary pluck would    start me rotting
sweet smelling and    slow at first
you could snip    me like a

stalk of foxgloves    and rest me
tilting in tapwater    in a green
glass vase you    could tear me
out by the    roots you might
catch the wild    allium scent while

walking me to    the bin maybe
taste my bitter    leaves maybe not
you could dismember    me petal by
petal procedurally modeling    someone else's love
there would be    nothing stopping you

Super 8 film    poem parts double
exposed living poem    to poem 69ing
or threewaying now    midwifing an extraterrestrial
fawn now juicing    all the hope
from a word    a flower's name

A Tribe Called    Quest is spawn
camping this jukebox    there's blue originated
outside the cosmos    on my left
nails a terrestrially    originated blue on
my right nails    responsibilities at home

sour thoughts all    day planets orrerying
around hugs being    passed despite everything
88 times per    second I feel
strongly that I'm    going to pay
for all this    at some point

tore a flap     of hand skin
off while climbing     came home did
some e-commerce caught     the half moon
through the skylight     reflected in the
glass of a     framed postcard from

Somerville Open Studios     sixish years ago
I was really     taken with this
guy's big claustrophobic     blue canvases astronauts
tangled in their     own oxygen lines
his name's probably     on the back

of the card     I could look
I'm only half     a paintings guy
I'm a whole     urgent problems in
space guy anyway     drank my teeth
brushed some water     went to bed

on each of      two days the
running was the      other day's task
the track was      a disheartening uphill
loop a cursed      naked AI video
loop kept coaxing      me back into

bed whispering admittedly      proficient sex sentences
the running was      slow going or
would've been if      I'd run any
it was loose      sand one step
sliding backwards every      step taken forwards

I'll run tomorrow      I thought yesterday
today I thought      I'll run yesterday
it was a      perfect system without
fault or fracture      a song smuggled
inside ceramic lorikeets      in a greenhouse

if I walk    the real sidewalk
all the way    to the garden
to pick raspberries    and if sunshine
slows and stops    at a depth
of an inch    or a half

into my shoulder    on the sunlit
side and if    real photons find
their spot there    warming the fibers
it will be    waking life celebrating
a week's reprieve    from dreaming's claims

on the truth    the veil and
vision of you    who might yet
scalpel me tingling    out of the
berry filled belly    even temporarily today
I'm happy to    let me pretend

it's either love    for what's given
or it's disavowal    nothing's in between
and a love    for what is
is too much    to endure most
of the time    a love that

can't but outlast    the given giving
way constantly from    firefly to light
to afterimage to    darkness it weighs
like nothing on    the agency of
the evaporating man    his garden of

snowdrops and hellebore    his fool's adrenaline
I want you    I'm wanting you
from outside myself    an airless moment
I'd wish to    have been there
feeling that feeling    changing the world

# REWRITE ANYTHING

guy on scaffold     again guy on
bridge again guy     on parking structure
again guy's same     momentary frozen silent
silhouette up on     water tower again
guy on communication     tower again guy

on overpass again     guy on ladder
on platform on     barn roof guy
on mushrooms on     scissor lift guy
on parapet guy     on buttress guy
on gargoyle again     guy back on

his bullshit again     guy on a
tear again guy     once again on
some inexplicable jag     guy up on
ceiling again guy     out on wing
again guy up     on balcony railing

and when you    write it again
let its answers    drum the fingers
of its questions    play the same
opening moves again    that same rhythm
you keep learning    to play at

the direct address    that one time
you walked off    the parking garage
right in front    of a train
that one time    you'll never live
it down the    memory's the wrong

key for the    remembering which makes
the compulsion to    press the play
button again all    the more vexing
and to tap    your fingers along
all the unexpected    spinal processes effortlessly

a wind-up whale    surfaced alongside me
it had stairs    for a tongue
a recorded voice    said "you're trespassing
I can swim    you back to
the visitors' area    here climb inside

the onboard entertainment    is a band
of mechanical mackerel    inside an aquarium
the band plays    the popular Peter
Gabriel song 'Sledgehammer'    you have to
stick your head    inside the aquarium

if you want    to hear them
you have to    feed them each
a token or    they won't play
tokens can be    purchased from the
clockwork pelican up    on the mezzanine"

bound up with words I misremembered
trapped in melody inside a device
of course the ear found it
bewildering the charge of the clouds
below gathering opposite the ground above

eventually yielded a sample of her
own voice sampled for music still
trapped in a handheld recorder she
is bewildered by the recorder's hand
familiar and routine and nothing seductive

about it and plainer even than
music this was 19 years ago
now loneliness she says rewind she
says sometimes I wield my loneliness
like strength is what I misremembered

once you've visited     a planet you'll
visit it again     once you hear
yourself use a     word it's impossible
to stop once     you trip over
a compelling sexual     fantasy you make

a mental note     on a faux-embroidery
recipe card and     you file it
by chronology in     the group sex
section in the     foursome subsection cross-referenced
by the participants'     names the birds

migrate up down     the salmon swim
long laps the     mind plays "96
Tears" every hour     on the hour
and races itself     400 meters around
even the unbounded     firmament of dreaming

the bus schedule's    wrong the vending
machine bill accepter    doesn't accept bills
occasionally a bone    escapes the skin
or an organ    turns inside out
there's a prolonged    war of attrition

with the insurance    company about who's
going to pay    for it and
when they win    they plant a
hilarious asparagus underneath    the pelvis which
pushes up impossibly    majestic intercepting the

sun the sundial    shadow sweeps days
over the growing    and withering daffodils
and daylilies and    dahlias that surround
the skull spine    femur humerus years
spilling into aeons    of fresh flowers

upside down spider    full of babies
abdomen bulging sad    smile "they're not
mine they're the    wasp's I'm not
a musician either    any longer I'm
a musical instrument    I'm a sampler"

I walk one    circle stepping stones
laid knowing exactly    once begun where
they are to    end a melody
of baby steps    plantigrade baby feet
so the parasite's    in the semen

which is flung    into the air
the wasp flies    through that and
stings the spider    the spider's in
the dream reconciling    the music stepwise
to the semen    and so on

# MUSEUM OF MEANING

sing it again      how a neonatal
ichthyosaur's bones came      to rest fossilized
in a story      among the bones
of some number      of adults how
little can be      known how you

count and characterize      the many phalanges
indistinguishable from pebbles      marching down the
forelimbs but you      can't say beyond
happenstance why the      individuals settled finally
where they settled      I'm trying to

make a photogrammetric      map of their
bed which will      eventually consist of
millions of triangular      faces the faces
will sing the      insufficient story and
the story will      nourish the parasite

the stillness of frogs and rhinos
lots of digital copies of enterprises
use machine learning the internal artifacts
disappear somewhere between the retina and
everybody else or say a gar

or a dangling salamander staged undyingly
afloat in space we reckon only
individuals we signal morphologies or camouflage
there's no consensus even after standardizing
the lighting and recounting the bones

lots of people look at the
integument at colorful takeaways call them
an ongoing effort a me sitting
inside inadequate glasses false color movies
a brain a repository of choice

I thought maybe     I'd rewrite the
constellations for you     I know we
don't know each     other well enough
for this I     thought the stars
could each belong     to any number

of constellations of     any size whether
a cricket singing     in the corner
or an orca     swallowing the sky
each star could     be like a
radical in a     character in any

number of words     accruing and imbuing
meaning equally and     dynamically when you
look up at     night you could
see the changes     waiting to be
written for you     or by you

they taught IS     first as in
intestine IS interior     something IS nobody
then other verbs     it messed me
up I make     it sound better
than it is     then they taught

other stuff and     I learned almost
some of it     it was easy
a transparent hummingbird     a diffraction cocktail
everything fell into     place and stayed
interior still IS     intestine and nobody

still IS something     sometimes it is
me and usually     there's a simple
word for it     I forgot the
other verbs I     willed them three
at a time     out of existence

I might be     a flight attendant
everyone is ignoring     my safety demonstration
I'm stuffing tail     first a snake
backwards into the     bag it sprung
out of it's     harder than it

looks this isn't     a real snake
of course but     it's been given
very lifelike movement     with servo motors
flexing all up     and down its
backbone and for     fangs quite venomous

fuel injectors a     snake does not
want to go     backwards into anything
it's a metaphor     a safety demonstration
the struggle to     convey its meaning
is very similar     to that meaning

don't read this      out of order
it's a description      or three dimensions
or three descriptions      or it's money
are museums money      are they words
are words data      one reads what

data doesn't say      one's data nests
inside data deeper      than one museum
or many inside      any museum's data
saying to moderns      in modern life
please check into      meaning for meanings

for meaning is      for everyday use
by real people      and professional users
and everyday individuals      species and populations
and all in      need of meaning
givers to give      them their meaning

they're going to    fire me if
I keep scrolling    back to this
jpeg of this    bluebird we just
had an earthquake    and Sam texted
me DID YOU    JUST FEEL THE

EARTHQUAKE I had    to think about
it for a    second it's a
mountain bluebird one    of my favorite
birds I have    this old memory
I saw one    for the first

time a tiny    rip a scrap
parting suddenly from    the sky on
a fencepost maybe    there are cosmic
downstream consequences every    time I remember
but it seems    like probably not

weakness of will    a downed tree
must simplify yourself    a lapsed word
a sound effect    met head on
assessment makes itself    in a day
decisions and roots    a decision tree

attractive subsurface scatter    on dedicated hardware
braindead dialog options    I was here
a complete infestation    where word was
think of me    in a typo
a parade route    into fallen trees

all the way    to the end
sing my song    or whatever's wanting
an illegible label    a shoebox collection
of fake parasite    life cycle diagram
watercolors with real    parasites in them

# REMEMBER ANYTHING

the main manifestation    of somatoparaphrenia is
the feeling of    disownership of the
contralesional body the    belief that contralesional
body parts do    not belong to
them but to    another person reinstatement

of ownership by    third-person perspective does
not permanently abolish    somatoparaphrenia suggesting that
the subjective sense    of body ownership
remains dominated by    an impaired first-person
representation of the    body that cannot

be updated patients    looking into the
mirror state that    the limb does
belong to them    however body ownership
of the limb    does not remain
after the mirror    is taken away

compare the picture      on the left
to the picture      on the right
is it before      and after are
there inexplicable differences      causal exemptions am
I dreaming again      is this that

catastrophic forgetting am      I still on
my side of      the river is
that blue rip      there I mean
beyond truly blue      retina problem blue
a surgeonfish darting      apparent as plastic

about among below      above along between
the rocks just      under the surface
two feet offshore      from anywhere in
this case Laguna      Garden Hotel Okinawa
79 years in      a nightmare's shadow

a pact I      wasn't part of
ivy up a      smokestack a mound
of bricks benches      sat in overgrown
fenced brown grass      approach lanes for
the car ferry      don't mistake process

for meaning some      billboards belying Eden
more bricks sanitation      trucks piles of
split logs a      new-looking platform a
poured concrete wall      some pink disintegrating
names an outcropping      of turtles a

greenhouse some overpasses      Residence Inn Dollar
Tree Shop Rite      Home Depot LA
Fitness black beige      and blue midsize
automobiles basking in      transparent sunshine electrical
substation graveyard hollow      warehouse tire center

drinking a bunch    of water (by
the way nothing    happens in this
one) like it's    that barium solution
or that colonoscopy    prep stuff I
cleaned up broken    glass at Waitts

Mountain with friends    I had beers
at Idle Hands    in Malden I
watched Ryan my    oldest friend play
Hades for a    while while the
beans for bean    soup cooked and

we laughed and    all that now
the soup's ready    my wife and
I are going    to watch one
standard unit of    Netflix tomorrow is
a Monday nothing    happens nothing happens

your daffodils came    up so perfect
again your lions    came up and
out without the    black blood around
their mouths again    your Mayans inherited
your selfies again    your dirt is

light a few    gajiillion microbes and
flatworms your patient    history is oddly
incomplete your gin    causes no hangovers
your mirrors once    again reflect so
perfectly only your    idea of a

mirror and we    talked about this
they do everything    you want a
mirror to do    and nothing you
don't you didn't    even notice but
I drink ink    so I noticed

the tedium is     perforated by pecks
and blips of     blissful absurdity remind
me to tell     you about the
morning we hoisted     the octopus model
in the stairwell     with climbing gear

actually that's basically     the whole story
the end of     the potato wedge
is dipped in     BBQ sauce and
then transferred to     the mouth I
let Northernlion or     Taskmaster play in

the background a     seagull impact silhouette
sticks to the     outside of a
pane of UV-resistant     window glass distant
supercomputer calculations quietly     remodel the rate
of ongoing species     loss per day

the heart wants      and even when
it gets it      it wants it
the tapeworm's a      tapeworm no inside
no outside it      drives a circulatory
system a Möbius      ribbon of ruby

taillights creeping along      a highway paved
globewise from here      to here binding
the possible the      grasping the friend's
life is given      summarily as "a
suicide" a moment      to live through

obscenity to have      lived through it
the sun shines      unbent sunshine down
on the state      murder of children
simple spiraling blood      remains of words
and up come      the hyacinths again

# WRITE ANYTHING

woke up writing     my heart was
still in halves     this was Wednesday
I dumped a     dozen eggs out
onto the store     floor like some
wacky sitcom robot     fully breaking nine

I exclaimed or     more accurately I
wrote an exclamation     point on a
Post-It I emailed     Elisa do you
want to see     something beautiful and
something beautiful was     hyperlinked to the

trailer for "Animal     Well" I handwrote
in ballpoint history's     moronic mudslide in
a gridlined spiralbound     notebook and typed
huey lewis i     want a new
drug in the     YouTube search bar

I hold three    cards Meaning Caution
and The Can    Opener I have
to play one    before the end
of my opponent's    turn the economy
of action in    this game is

unusual I keep    thinking about what
Meaning would mean    specifically whether it
would mean meaning    or something specific
to the game    today I looked
at a complement    of clouds I

did some e-commerce    I nosed pistachio
shells into letter    shapes if Meaning
is out then    Caution is too
so it's The    Can Opener and
that's how easy    this game is

here it comes    the lyric moment
I go crashing    through a thorny
hedge that wasn't    there a second
ago to get    my camera and
the eclipse ends    as it begins

now it's later    I'm hearing various
starlings speaking unreality    into their pasts
or letting unreality    speak unreality out
of its present    the zinnia petals
to my left    acquire texture around

their edges through    my reading glasses
a pink woven    from pink threads
an idea's hem    you could peck
a self-disclosing seeming    like a thing
you'd forget you'd    been born knowing

I'm finally filling     my water bottle
my hands shaking     are doing everything
not to help     I know you
wrote me last     and after I
write you and     you write me

again you will     have written me
last again and     again I try
imagining the moment     a probe going
in through the     elbow and down
along the ulna     and tugging the

finger tendons to     write what's written
all the crumbs     and lint and
shit that got     into the gaps
between this moment     this imaginary moment
and the moments     before and after

I mark twentysomething    emails as read
I answer an    email about safety
training in one    of the imaging
facilities I write    an email to
try to provoke    action on the

delivery of the    instrument we ordered
I answer another    email saying yes
we can meet    to talk about
fabricating a tray    any day but
Tuesday is usually    good I respond

to another email    indicating that the
doorway is 40    inches wide with
swing-clear hinges I    restart "Standstill" by
Disasterpeace I approve    people's time reports
and I do    a little e-commerce

I'm as light	as a spasming
transparent jellyfish bell	which I stow
my wishes in	without wishing them
and which floats	transparently away pulsing
along the Acheron	across the Lethe

I move with	perfect grace I
climb with effortless	beauty with love
piloting my senses	I hear air
deafening music I	climb what isn't
there I hear	swallows whispering past

I acknowledge some	pain I understand
my heart rate	I breathe deep
I plan I	make corporeal plans
before moving I	climb illusion with
abandon I breathe	again and again

juneberries in daylight    on the far
daylit riverbank where    a general's said
to have called    his soldiers on
this side by    name from memory
so they'd know    they could cross

without entering oblivion    statues stand in
where they stood    I've been thinking
about sugar cookies    a little bit
something simple like    a sugar cookie
can add a    bit of joy

to one's day    the sun paints
a stripe overhead    one nudges letters
around making glib    sense of darkness
dark letters on    white daylit paper
blandest of things    the daylit thing

# ONLY OCCASIONS

I drank a     grape soda today
I don't remember     the last time
Elisa and John     were alive there
in the city     where they live
I found this     almost perfect desaturated

blue nail polish     easy to love
a color on     a day like
today the wind     came all this
way just to     braid you up
between its fingers     you might extend

that kind of     grace to yourself
and who else's     but your own
fingers or anyone's     to imagine in
the wind's fragile     stead whose sensate
fingertips tangled in     a new dragonfly

my friend Yonatan    was biking along
and suddenly found    himself giving incorrect
answers to paramedics    what year how
old they towed    him half listing
to the same    emergency room where

he'd worked twelve    hour shifts as
a resident surrounded    by shades being
sorted and attended    to in varying
ways and degrees    of apparent urgency
some seats sat    unfilled within him

while doctors walked    and walked through
this windowless place    he went home
as always before    on the T
climbing up the    exit stairs pressing
his feet again    against the asphalt

I'm a flight    attendant the passengers
brought their own    plexiglass window cutting
kits on board    FAA regulations stipulate
that I have    to make them
throw them out    the windows but

this is in    your honor they
say and then    one of them
definitely someone important    to me stands
up and says    Surprise it's a
surprise funeral for    me and it's

really moving and    really touching they're
eating those radioactive    green pistachio cookies
which I always    really loved they
even knew to    play the Deerhoof
At My Funeral    playlist I made

I failed    it seems    to hear
the end    of the    long diminuendo
of the    chimes which    Bill and
Pen made    in intervals    of the
harmonic series    and which    Bill shook

once after    he'd finished    mowing the
lawn and    stared at    as flies
buzzed all    around and    a sound
impossible to    relive overtook    the afternoon
before he    walked off    somewhere else

and now    I hear    one hermit
thrush calling    it's my    favorite sound
and flies    and the    rolling of
the road    and the    leaves whispering
to themselves    having reached    uneasy consensus

I took the     wrong way and
then the long     way here but
here I am     while Sam goes
over the ceremony     with you guys
I think it     was winter wrens

I was hearing     singing after the
train driver yinzerly     asked me hey'd
jyou pay? and     dropped me at
Belasco which apparently     is a name
given to like     eight squares of

sidewalk the redbud     and all spring
pops open tomorrow     the day after
nobody can say     except you'll be
married which will     be a way
to have said     which is good

all the shadows  flash green flashing
sunlight and birdsong  smelly growing things
laughing at our  perfect private jokes
we kissed each  other and breakfast
we planted our  mighty eggplant and

tomato seedlings and  some suspect sunflowers
I bought a  maroon shirt for
un dólar the  sky is everyone's
to condense however  they may oh
what could survive  such maudlin such

grand perihelial schmoop  the gravity whip
speeds the little  spacecraft away wherever
we showered and  swallowed cold green
soup and leftover  cauliflower pizza and
we're on a  train to Providence

is it one      or many contentments
I received the      messages I left
myself and I      deleted some others
also from me      one must simply
record every occurrence      with best fidelity

today you called      me into the
bedroom to see      the sunset again
the wall of      daylight in front
of the face      fades and all
the graffiti slides      off and all

the time lately      when I see
you in profile      somewhere in thought
I catch myself      thinking this moment
is the one      I'll remember forever
as though I      could just choose

fast asleep in    a spent parachute
that I'd slung    from a beam
in an unfinished    part of the
house where nobody    would find me
I don't even    know quite where

just asleep just    ultimately a lump
a sunlit orange    and yellow cocoon
stalled out in    its descent a
few inches above    the floor it's
all the being    I have today

a beautiful gift    with about half
the day left    I keep thinking
about the glow    through the eyelids
he's not seeing    where did he
go and where    is he going

# Notes/Acknowledgements

I want to thank Elaine Bleakney, MaryCat Boyett, Emily Braker, Sommer Browning, Verity Burke, David Cameron, Heather Christle, John Cotter, Anne Everly, Elisa Gabbert, Isabel Galleymore, Yonatan Grad, Brendan Haley, Patrick Hargon, Helena Hunter, Stevie Kennedy-Gold, Ann & Kirby Kenny, Natan Last, Lesle Lewis, Laura Mullen, Ben Musher, Sam Musher, Geoffrey Nutter, Benjamin Paloff, Ben Pease, Sarah Rankin, Matthew Rohrer, Zach Stern, KC Trommer, Andrew Weatherhead, and Wendy Xu.

Thanks also to the editors of *Apartment Poetry* for publishing five pieces from the REWRITE ANYTHING section.

The text on page 53 comes from the Wikipedia article on Somatoparaphrenia (accessed on April 17th, 2024 and March 22nd, 2025) and is used here under a CC BY-SA 4.0 license.